LCHF SIMPLE GUIDE

JOANNA ALDERSON

PHOTO INTRODUCTION

Think LCHF food has to be boring? Think again!

Here is just a sampling of some of the great food you will get to eat on this plan:

spaghetti & meat sauce

Waffle Pizza

Orange Chicken

Berries & Cream

INTRODUCTION

With the popularity of healthy "real food" eating on the rise (especially the low carb movement and the Paleo movement) people are now interested in looking for other healthy options to heal their bodies from a lifetime dependency on sugar and grains.

Dr. Andreas Enfeldt has the most popular diet website in Sweden, and has been very instrumental in changing that country's population into a fat eating rather than a carb eating nation.

He also has an English subscription website www.dietdoctor.com.which is very popular, and where he shares many informational interviews and videos as well as articles, recipes, and much more.

This book is based on his teachings.

I want to make it clear that this book is NOT endorsed by Dr. Eenfeldt. In fact, chances are he doesn't even know of it's existence.

I started out writing it for myself as a way to keep track

of all the notes I made from watching his videos and listening to his interviews, but since many of my readers have told me they are also interested in Low Carb High Fat, I have decided to make my notes available in ebook form so others can benefit from them as well.

However that being said, everything you will find in this book is purely my understanding of Dr. Eenfeldt's teachings.

It's not gospel.

Even though I have tried to be very careful in checking my material, I might have made mistakes, therefore I suggest you use this as only a quick easy introduction, and look to Dr. Eenfeldt's books, video, podcasts and especially his website for the final word on the subject.

By following Dr. Eenfeldt's recommendations I have found it surprisingly easy to become a fat burner, and I've had great results. I hope this book with help you be just as successful with your own dieting efforts.

WHAT IS LCHF

What is LCHF? It's a plan that basically turns the normally recommended American diet upside down.

THE DIETARY GUIDELINES that are presently in place in the US (the My Plate guidelines) recommend that the basis of your diet be carbs, followed by protein, and then a minimum amount of fat.

THE LCHF DIET asks you to do the opposite. The basis of the LCHF diet is fat. This is supplemented with adequate protein - not too much, just adequate - and a few carbs, mainly from leafy green vegetables.

THIS IS A COMPLETELY different way of eating, and most Americans will find this a very foreign concept, but in many parts of the world now it's become accepted as the much better way.

And since the countries where this is an acceptable way of eating tend to have a much healthier overall population, it only makes sense that there might be something to it.

IN THIS BOOK, with the help of the notes I've taken while following top LCHF advocate Dr. Eenfeld, I will explain exactly how it's done, how to deal with any problems or concerns you might have, and what specific foods and recipes you can eat.

THE DIFFERENCE BETWEEN
LCHF & KETO

This can be very confusing for a lot of people.

It's a very common mistake to assume they are both the same plan, after all, at first glance they seem that way. Both ways of eating are high fat, moderate protein and low carb.

But there *is* a big difference, and that difference is Ketones and Ketosis.

WHEN YOU DO A KETOGENIC DIET, you are pushing your body to burn fat and measuring that it does so by keeping track of the ketones in your blood.

When you do LCHF you are not as strict.

You eat a high fat and minimal carb diet, but whether or not you are actually in ketosis doesn't matter.

For most people, the plan will still work even if you're body never gets to ketosis.

THE DIFFERENCE IS NOT SO MUCH in the method, as it is in how strictly you follow it.

When you're LCHF you have more leeway. You can eat a bit more carbs as long as you are basically eating a high fat diet.

SO A KETO DIET is always an LCHF diet, but an LCHF diet is not always a KETO diet.

Moving on to KETO is the next step to take if LCHF doesn't work as well for you as you would like.

LCHF BENEFITS

What are the benefits of doing an LCHF diet? You can divide them up into 3 different areas.

FIRST, the LCHF diet is used as as medical therapy for many medical conditions, some of which are quite serious. These include :
- Obesity
- Heart burn
- Fatty liver disease
- Diabetes
- Polycystic ovary syndrome (causes infertility in women)
- Irritable bowel syndrome

THE LCHF DIET can also be preventive.

Studies are presently being done looking into preventing dementia with an LCHF diet.

. . .

FINALLY, the LCHF diet is a great diet for just about anyone, even if they are healthy with no medical conditions.

People on a low carb diet report loss of hunger and cravings, and more energy.

PART ONE
HOW TO EAT LCHF

In this section I'm going to give you some of the general guidelines for eating an LCHF diet given by Dr. Eenfeld on his website.

GENERAL RULES

So how do you eat LCHF? Here is the general rule :

When you're hungry, eat Real foods - few carbs and lots of fat - until you're satisfied.

YOU DON'T HAVE to count calories, go hungry, take any pills or eat any diet products. All you need is real food.

DO CALORIES COUNT? Yes, but you don't usually need to count them because the LCHF diet is so satisfying you usually eat less than what you're used to eating and are still satisfied.

It's only if you find that you're not meeting your weight-less goals that it's helpful to track exactly what you're eating.

And usually you will find that the problem isn't with the right foods, it's the wrong foods.

. . .

HOW ABOUT CARBS? Do you need to count these?

Yes, but if you stick to the basic beginner's rule - eat only foods with less than 5% carbs - that will be sufficient.

WHAT TO EAT

So what are the right foods ?

Meat and Poultry, seafood, eggs, vegetables, and natural fats and sauces.

MEAT AND POULTRY

Choose what you like. Beef, pork, poultry, bacon - they are all good.

The fatty parts are good for you and so is the skin on the chicken.

Choose organic and grass fed if you can. These foods taste better and are also better for your health.

SEAFOOD

You can eat any kind of seafood, but fatty fish such as salmon and sardines are especially good.

Avoid anything with breading since this will contain too many carbs.

Wild caught fish is the healthiest if you can get it.

. . .

EGGS

These are a perfect and nutritious food, especially if you eat organic free-range eggs.

How many can you eat? Dr. Eenfeldt has been known to tell people to eat no more than 36 eggs a day - but it's okay to eat less!

VEGETABLES

When it comes to vegetables the simple rule is eat vegetables that grow above ground and avoid those that grow below ground.

You can eat a pound a day of above ground vegetables with no problem, and this will give you all the vitamins and minerals you need. (See the vegetables section for more specific guidelines.)

FATS AND SAUCES

Use real butter and heavy cream for cooking.

You can have rich sauces like Bernaise and Hollandaise.

You can also use garlic butter, coconut oil, and olive oil. These are all excellent choices.

Avoid vegetable oils such as canola and soy oil.

NATURALLY RICH DAIRY products are also good. Eat real cheese and high fat yogurt - at least 17% fat. However dairy products still contain some milk sugar, so be careful not to over eat these.

. . .

HOW MUCH FAT can you eat? Dr. Eenfeldt says "Eat until you're satisfied, and if you're hungry, eat more fat."

SPECIAL **Occasions**

What can you have for treats?

Nuts make a great snack. (See the nuts section for more specific guidelines.) You can also have a small piece of dark chocolate (at least 65%) on occasion.

EXCEPT FOR SPECIAL OCCASIONS, you should avoid all fruit except for berries.

A few berries with whipped cream is okay, and is a popular LCHF dessert. (See the fruit section for more specific guidelines.)

DRINKS

What should you drink?

The best is plain water - either regular or carbonated. You can also flavor it with lemon, lime or some cucumber slices.

Coffee and tea is also okay. You can use as bit of heavy whipped cream in your coffee, but avoid milk.

YOU CAN ALSO HAVE a glass of wine or other non-sugar drink on occasion. (See the alcohol section for more specific guidelines.)

WHAT NOT TO EAT

What foods should you avoid?
- Sugar and foods with sugar in them
- Sweets such as candy, cookies and cakes made with sugar
- Starchy foods such as pasta, rice and potatoes
- Low fat dairy products. These contain tons of sugar

THESE FOODS all contain lots of carbs.

THE WORST THINGS for your weight and health are soda and fruit juice.

This includes sports drinks and energy bombs. These are all sugar bombs and you should definitely avoid them.

ALSO AVOID BEER.

It's full of rapidly digested carbs. There is a reason why they call it a "Beer Belly"!

. . .

WHY SHOULD you avoid starchy foods?

These contain long chains of glucose, As they reach the stomach, they rapidly convert to pure glucose, which raises your blood sugar and shuts down your fat burning.

LASTLY, you should avoid fruit. It contains lost of sugar. View it as nature's candy and have it only occasionally.

ALCOHOL

Can you drink alcohol on LCHF?

Sure, in moderate amounts, but beer and sweet drinks need to be avoided.

Choose wine or non-sweetened liquor.

ALSO REMEMBER that alcohol is not a weight loss aid. The more you drink, the more weight loss may slow down as the body burns the alcohol before anything else.

MOST PEOPLE on an LCHF diet choose wine or pure spirits (without the sweet mixers) when they want a drink.

Here are the approximate amount of carbs per serving (1 glass) of popular LCHF drinks :

0 CARBS : whiskey, martini, brandy, tequila shot

1 carb : champagne

4 carbs : red wine, white wine

FRUIT

If you want to get the maximum fat-burning effect from your LCHF diet, avoid all fruit other than berries.

Most people on an LCHF diet eat fruit only occasionally as a treat.

HERE ARE the approximate net carb counts (total carbs minus fibre) for some of the most common fruits :

FOR 100 GRAMS or 3.5 ounces :
  5 carbs: rasberries, Blackberries
  6 carbs : strawberries

These can be eaten in small amounts on a strict LCHF diet. If you're on a more moderate diet you can eat all you want.

THE FOLLOWING FRUIT has a lot more carbs and should be eaten very rarely (if at all) and in small amounts :

. . .

FOR 100 GRAMS or 3.5 ounces :

6 carbs: coconut meat, lemon

7 carbs: cantaloupe, Plums

9 carbs: peaches

10 carbs: watermelon, Clementines, Cherries, Oranges

12 carbs: blueberries, Kiwi fruit, Apples, Pears, Pineapple

13 carbs: mango

16 carbs: grapes

20 carb : banana

NUTS

Nuts make a great LCHF snack but you can't eat an unlimited amount because they still contain carbs.

However some kinds of nuts are lower than others. As you can see by the list below, pistachios and cashews should be avoided.

A tip for moderating your intake is to make sure you measure out a serving before you start eating.

Don't eat straight out of the bag!

Also, studies have shown that salted nuts are harder to stop eating than unsalted nuts, so try to avoid these.

FOR 100 GRAMS or 3.5 ounces:

4 carbs: pecans, Brazil nuts
5 carbs: macadamia nuts
7 carbs: hazelnuts, Walnuts, Peanuts
9 carbs: pine nuts
10 carbs: almonds
18 carbs: pistachios
27 carbs: cashews

VEGETABLES

The basic rule is eat vegetables that grow above ground freely, and those that grow below ground sparingly.

As you can see by the list below, all potatoes have tons of carbs and should be avoided.

HERE ARE the carb counts for a 100 grams or 3.5 ounce serving :

ABOVE GROUND VEGETABLES
1 carb: spinach
2 carbs: avocado, Lettuce, Asparagus
3 carbs: cucumber, Olives, Eggplant, Tomato, Zucchini, Cabbage, Green peppers
4 carbs: cauliflower, Kale, Broccoli, Red peppers
5 carbs: brussels sprouts, Yellow peppers

BELOW GROUND VEGETABLES

7 grams: carrots, Onions, Beets, Rutabaga, Celery root
9 carbs: peas
15 grams: potatoes, Corn
16 grams: baked beans
17 grams: sweet potatoes

PART TWO
TIPS FOR WEIGHT LOSS

Now that you've got the basic information, I'm sure there are still some questions you have about the LCHF diet.

How much should you eat? What else is important ? These and other questions will be answered in this section.

CARBS

One of the biggest mistakes new LCHF dieter make is eating too many carbs. Here are Dr. Andreas Eenfeldt's guidelines :

For maximum effects, keep to a **Strict LCHF diet - below 20 grams of carbs a day**

For a decent effect, keep to a **Moderate LCHF diet - 20 to 50 grams of carbs a day**

SOME OF THE biggest offenders are consuming fruit and beer. These can up your carb count dramatically.

To avoid eating too many carbs, use an online tool to track your carbs until you have a good idea of what foods you can and can't eat to keep within your guidelines.

WHEN AND HOW MUCH TO EAT

It's very important on this plan to **eat only when you are hungry,** and when you do eat, to **eat until you are full.**

IF YOU EAT EVEN if you're not hungry, you'll probably maintain your weight, but you won't lose any, so if weight-loss is your goal, keep this in mind.

IT'S important to eat to satiety, because constant hunger eats away at your self discipline and makes you tired.

This is when you're likely to give up.

EATING until you are fun provides long lasting satiety and reduces sugar cravings.

On LCHF you can eat less and still be satisfied, and it becomes easier to skip the bad stuff.

· · ·

IF YOU ARE CONSTANTLY CRAVING and you need to eat all the time, there is something wrong.

Probably you need to eat more fat.

SO EAT when you're hungry until you are full, but, just as important, if you want to become lean don't eat if you're not hungry.

Needless snacking will definitely stall your weightless.

MOST COMMONLY OVEREATEN FOODS

There are 3 common traps to watch out for on the LCHF diet :

(1) DAIRY PRODUCTS

When you're eating products like cream and cheese, it's very easy to keep eating even when you're not hungry just because they taste good.

Especially if you drink a lot of coffee with cream, remember all these cups can add up to a lot of extra carbs.

Some people think they can snack on unlimited cheese, and this is a mistake. All dairy products still contain some carbs.

(2) **Nuts**

Like with cream and cheese, it's too easy to keep eating nuts even when you're not hungry, just because they taste so good.

Also, salted nuts can be very addictive, and if you sit

down in from on the TV with a bag of nuts, you will find that you have eaten the whole bag without even realizing it.

That's why you should always portion them out before you start eating.

(3) LOW CARB BAKED GOODS

Being able to make low carb baked goods can be very helpful when you miss things like bread, but it's very easy to overdo these.

Especially desserts.

Snacking on low carb desserts when you're not hungry will definitely slow down your weight loss.

Weight

Contrary to most common recommendations, Dr. Eenfeld wants you to keep track of your weight on a regular basis, in fact several times a day.

It's not enough to just measure once a week, because your weight will go up and down several times a day - sometimes as much as 5 lbs in the same day.

DR. EENFELDT RECOMMENDS you get a wireless scale. This will send information directly to your computer and enable you to see graphs at a moment's notice. Then you can just hop onto the scale a few times a day, whenever you think of it.

WHEN YOU ARE READING the results it's important to look at the overall trend over time, not the weight on any given day.

There are two reasons why he says to weight yourself regularly :

(1) IT'S great motivation to see that what you're doing is working. This will keep you going.

(2) IF WHAT you're doing is NOT working, it's good to find out as soon as possible so you can do something about it as soon as possible.

MEASUREMENTS

HE ALSO RECOMMENDS you measure your waistline since this is also a great measure of your health. Here are the recommended measurements you should aim for :

OKAY EXCELLENT

MEN < 40" < 37"
    < 102 cm < 94 cm

WOMEN < 34.5 " < 321.5 "
    < 88 cm < 80 cm

SLEEP

Lots of people today suffer from sleep depravation and think this is normal.

The problem with lack of sleep is that it doesn't just make you tired and sluggish, it also makes you fatter.

It increases abdominal fat.

It makes you hungrier.

It makes you crave sweets.

Sleep depravation is a total disaster for self discipline. It makes it easy for you to fall for any temptation that comes your way.

THE GOOD NEWS is you can become smarter, improve your self discipline, and lose weight just by going to bed earlier.

HOW MUCH SLEEP makes you feel you're best and makes you your leanest? The answer is sleeping until you wake up spontaneously.

On average this means about 8 hours per day. It varies between 7 to 9 hours, but not less than 7.

TO KEEP track of your sleep you can try the app Sleep Cycle which is available for both iPhone and Android.

You put your phone under your pillow, and you get stats on how you slept. You can also see what improves and impairs your sleep.

GETTING the sleep you need is an investment in a better life and a leaner body.

INTERMITTENT FASTING

Intermittent Fasting is a good option to add to your LCHF plan if you're not getting the results you want from the diet alone.

Often women over forty have the most difficulty losing weight, and Intermittent fasting can make a big difference.

When you combine Intermittent Fasting with LCHF, fasting is easier and burns more fat.

THERE ARE many variations that you can try, but here are the two that Dr. Eenfeld recommends :

THE 5:2 **Diet**

On this diet you eat to satiety five days a week, then for the other two days you eat a minimal calorie diet. (500 calories for women, 600 calories for men.)

A lot of people choose Saturday and Sunday for this fast, but these days don't need to be together.

They can be any days of the week that are most convenient for you - for example Tuesday and Thursday.

THE 16:8 **Diet**

This is the version that Dr. Eenfeldt uses himself. You never have to count calories or weight food. All you do is fast for 16 hours every day and then eat during an 8 hour window.

THE EASIEST WAY TO do this is to stop eating after dinner - for example by 8 pm - then skip breakfast (maybe have a cup of coffee instead) and then eat lunch any time after noon the next day.

YOU CAN DO this 16 hour fast a few times a week or every day.

The more often, the more effective it will be. Keep eating good food when you're hungry except when you're fasting.

SIMPLE, time-saving, and effective for your weight.

PART THREE
MOST COMMON LCHF PROBLEMS

Just as with anything else, people sometimes have problems when they start the LCHF diet.

These usually are not severe, but you can minimize them if you know how.

In this section I'll cover some of the most common problems.

INDUCTION FLU

Some people, when they first start the LCHF diet, develop flu-like symptoms during days 2 to 4 of the plan. Headache, feeling tired, lethargic and unmotivated, nausea, brain fog and irritability are all common symptoms of Induction Flu.

The main cause is usually dehydration and/or salt deficiency, which is caused by a temporary increase in urination.

THE BEST CURE is to dissolve half a teaspoon of salt in a glass of water and drink this.

If your symptoms disappear within 15 to 30 minutes, then you will know that is what it was. You can do this once a day for the first week.

YOU CAN ELIMINATE SUFFERING from the Induction Flu completely by making a couple of cups of chicken, beef or bone broth a part of your diet from day one.

Just make sure it's not low salt, as adding back the salt you need is the whole point of this intervention.

YOU ALSO NEED to make sure you're getting enough fat. The easiest way? Just add butter to whatever you're eating.

LEG CRAMPS

Leg cramps are a side effect of the loss of magnesium due to increased urination. To avoid them :
   • Drink plenty of liquids and get enough salt.
   • If needed, supplement with magnesium.
   Take 3 slow release magnesium tablets a day for 20 days, then continue taking 1 a day afterwards (This recommendation is from the Art & Science of Low Carb Living.)
   Remember to check with your doctor before taking any supplements.

CONSTIPATION

Constipation is a common side effect, but can easily be dealt with:

- Drink plenty of liquids and get enough salt.
- Eat plenty of non starchy vegetables
- If necessary, add fibre in the form of psyllium seed husks dissolved in water.
- If none of the above works, take some Milk of Magnesia

BAD BREATH

Some people, when they've been doing LCHF for a while, find that they start to suffer from bad breath.

The smell is from acetone, a ketone body.

TO DEAL with it use a breath freshener regularly, or chew on some sugar-free breath mints.

AS A LAST RESORT you can try upping your carb consumption, but this might slow down your weightless.

HEART PALPITATIONS

When starting an LCHF diet some people complain about suddenly developing heart palpitations.

This is nothing to be worried about.

It's perfectly normal and usually disappears once your body is used to the diet. The important thing is to make sure you drink lots of liquids and get enough salt.

IF YOU ARE REALLY WORRIED, make sure you check with your doctor.

PART FOUR
12 BASIC LCHF RECIPES

This is not a recipe book, but to make it simple for you to get started right away I'm including some of my favorite basic LCHF recipes.

With these twelve basic recipes you can start your diet and eat tasty satisfying meals until you have time to find other recipes you like better.

And if that doesn't happen ... well it probably doesn't matter.

Even though many people love looking through recipes, most people tend to eat the same half a dozen meals over and over again.

There is nothing wrong with that. In fact, it can make your life a heck of a lot simpler!

KETO WAFFLES

These waffles are great for a weekend breakfast or brunch or as a bread substitute for sandwiches. I also use them to make Keto Danish and a great Waffle Pizza.

These are extremely simple to make. All you do is blend 2 ingredients together and your batter is ready.

YOU WILL NEED a waffle iron to make these, but if you're planning to stay on this plan it will be a good investment because you're going to be using it very frequently.

You can get a waffle iron on Amazon for about $30, so they aren't that expensive. Just make sure you get a non-stick one.

MAKES 6 large waffles (24 quarters)

INGREDIENTS:
    8 free-range eggs
    8 oz. Organic Cream cheese

DIRECTIONS:
    - Put the cream cheese into your blender and break the eggs on top of it.
    - Blend the eggs and cheese until you get a thin bubbly batter.
    - The batter needs to rest, so this is when to preheat your waffle iron for 5 minutes.
    - Once the waffle iron is hot, pour enough of the batter in to almost cover all the holes, then using a knife, gently move the batter around until it fills the open ones. Be careful not to pour in too much batter or it will leak out of the sides.
    - Now close the lid and wait until you no longer see any steam. (About 5 minutes.)
    - Gently remove with a non-stick spatula and put on a plate to cool.

- Once they are completely cool, put in a freezer bag and freeze.

- To serve, thaw the waffles and toast them. (I do this in my toaster oven and they crisp up very nicely.)

GREEN SALAD WITH VINAIGRETTE

This is a great basic mainstay salad that can be made any number of ways.

IN THIS VERSION I use a lot of baby spinach with

avocado and bacon. I also sometimes turn it into a Chef's salad by adding bits of leftover protein and a boiled egg.

On special occasions I make the salad with endive and radicchio leaves and serve it with a Champagne vinaigrette. (See below)

MAKES 1 serving

INGREDIENTS:
    2 cups salad greens
    1/2 avocado
    Basic vinaigrette
    1 slice crispy cooked bacon chopped into small pieces

DIRECTIONS:
    - Line your salad plate with greens.
    - Chop the avocado and sprinkle over the greens.
    - Drizzle with vinaigrette.
    - Sprinkle with the bacon bits and serve.

BASIC VINAIGRETTE

INGREDIENTS:
    1/4 cup of vinegar (Apple cider or Champagne) or lemon juice
    3/4 cup of extra virgin olive oil
    1 tablespoon chopped fresh herbs

1/2 teaspoon Dijon mustard (optional)
Salt and freshly ground pepper

DIRECTIONS:
- Put all the ingredients other than the oil into a blender and blend until well combined.
- Keeping the blender running, add the oil slowly until you've added the whole amount.

YOU CAN ALSO MAKE this by putting everything into a salad dressing bottle and giving it a good shake.

CAULIFLOWER MASH

This is a great replacement for mashed potatoes. Each serving is only half a cup (It's very rich) so one cauliflower will give you a lot of servings.

MAKES 6 to 8 servings

INGREDIENTS:

1 medium head of cauliflower washed and cut into large pieces

1/4 cup of butter

1/4 cup grated Cheddar cheese
Salt and freshly ground black pepper to taste
Grated parmesan for serving

DIRECTIONS:

- Steam the cauliflower pieces (on the stove or in the microwave) until very tender.

- Puree the cooked cauliflower in a food processor or blender.

- Add the butter, Cheddar, salt and pepper and blend again.

- Divide into portions and freeze.

TO SERVE:

Place one portion of the thawed cauliflower into a small greased individual custard cup, sprinkle with 1 tablespoon of grated parmesan, then heat in a 400'F oven for 10 –15 minutes until the top has browned. (I use the toaster oven for this and heat it the same time I heat my main course.)

WAFFLE PIZZA

This is a really easy recipe. Keto waffles make a great crispy thin crust pizza that's not floppy. You can eat it with your fingers just like a regular pizza.

BELOW I'M GOING to give you three of my favorite toppings, but you can use any toppings you like. Any toppings you would put on a regular pizza you can also use with a waffle pizza.

IN ORDER TO get a crispy crust on the finished pizza, I make it in two steps.

On Cook Ahead day I make the waffles for the crusts, cool them completely, then freeze them.

On pizza day I take my half waffle out of the freezer, unwrap it, and let it thaw, unwrapped, in the fridge until I need it. This lets it dry out a bit and helps the crust to stay crispy.

MAKES 1 large or 2 small servings

INGREDIENTS:

PEPPERONI & Olive Pizza

1 Keto waffle

3 tablespoons low sugar pizza sauce (I use EDEN organic pizza and pasta sauce)

1/4 - 1/2 teaspoon crushed hot pepper flakes (optional)

1 teaspoon Pizza seasoning (or Italian seasoning)

2 ounces of organic mozzarella shredded

1/4 cup of organic parmesan grated

6 large black olives cut in half

10 slices of Faction & Morello pepperoni (or your favorite brand)

. . .

VEGETARIAN Pizza

1 Keto waffle

3 tablespoons low sugar pizza sauce

1/4 – 1/2 teaspoon crushed hot pepper flakes (optional)

1 teaspoon Pizza seasoning (or Italian seasoning)

2 ounces of organic mozzarella shredded

1/4 cup organic parmesan grated

6 large black olives cut in half

1/2 cup of chopped broccoli

1/2 cup of chopped mushrooms

EVERYTHING PIZZA

1 Keto waffle

3 tablespoons low sugar pizza sauce

1/4 – 1/2 teaspoon crushed hot pepper flakes (optional)

1 teaspoon Pizza seasoning (or Italian seasoning)

2 ounces of organic mozzarella shredded

1/4 cup organic parmesan grated

6 large black olives cut in half

10 slices of Faction & Morello pepperoni (or your favorite brand)

1/2 cup of chopped broccoli

1/2 cup of chopped mushrooms

YOU CAN SUBSTITUTE or add anything else you like - ground beef, bacon, sausage, etc.

DIRECTIONS:

- Heat your oven to 425'F. Meanwhile toast the waffle and allow it to cool so it gets nice and crispy.

- Spray or brush one side of the waffle with olive oil, then place it oiled side down on a parchment lined pan.

- Top with pizza sauce, seasonings, mozzarella, and half the parmesan.

- Add the rest of the toppings, ending with the olive halves, then sprinkle with the rest of the parmesan.

- Put in the hot oven and bake for 8 to 10 minutes, just until the cheese has melted.

ASIAN NOODLES & SHRIMP

This recipe uses Miracle Noodles to make a delicious filling dish that will satisfy your cravings for Chinese food.

You can vary the basic recipe to make it a complete meal by adding chopped vegetables or make it more filling by adding bits of protein like cooked shrimp, chicken, beef or pork. (The photo above shows Asian Noodles with Shrimp & Snow Peas)

The gelatin powder will add lots of protein already, but you can also leave this out if you want.

Makes 1 serving

INGREDIENTS:

1 package angel hair Miracle Noodles
1 cup bone broth
1 tablespoon gelatin powder (optional, but will give you more protein if you need it)
1 teaspoon Sriracha sauce
1 teaspoon toasted sesame oil
1 tablespoon Soy sauce
Pinch ground ginger
Pinch garlic powder

DIRECTIONS:

- In a medium saucepan mix together the bone broth, gelatin powder, Sriracha sauce, Soy sauce ginger and garlic powders. Don't worry if the gelatin floats on the top. It will gradually dissolve as the sauce heats.

- Place on high heat and bring to a boil.

- Meanwhile open the bag of noodles, strain in a sieve over the sink, then rinse well with warm water. (About 2 minutes) Cut a few times with scissors so the strands of pasta aren't too long.

- Add the strained noodles to the sauce and keep boiling, watching all the time, until the sauce cooks down and becomes thick and coats the noodles. You don't want any liquid to be left on the bottom of the pan.

   - Remove and pour into a bowl. Drizzle the toasted sesame oil over the top before serving.

HERBED SALMON

This is a great basic recipe for preparing salmon. Once it's cooked you can serve it many ways.

IF YOU ENJOY the taste of salmon, just eat it cooked with

a little lemon juice and butter, or cold with a dollop of mayo.

If you're not crazy over the taste, you have several alternatives.

SERVE it cold in warm weather with a spicy mayonnaise or with Citrus Salsa.

In cold weather Parmesan Butter Sauce will go perfectly. All these sauces will mask most of the salmon taste, and you'll still be getting all the nutrients. (see below for the recipes.)

MAKES 4 servings

INGREDIENTS:
4 - 4 oz. Wild Salmon fillets (without skin)
1 tablespoon chopped garlic (or 1 teaspoon garlic powder)
1 tablespoon olive oil
2 tablespoons lemon juice (fresh is best)
1/2 teaspoon chopped fresh dill (or 1/4 teaspoon dry)
1/2 teaspoon chopped fresh parsley (or 1/4 teaspoon dry)
1/2 teaspoon chopped fresh tarragon (or 1/4 teaspoon dry)

DIRECTIONS:
- Preheat oven to 325'F

- Combine all the ingredients in a small bowl and mix well.

- Line a baking pan with parchment or non-stick foil and place the fillets evenly over the bottom so they don't overlap.

- Spread the herb mixture evenly over the top of the salmon.

- Bake for 15 to 20 minutes, or until the fish flakes easily with a fork.

FOR THE CITRUS SALSA:

Makes 4 servings (See photo above)

INGREDIENTS:

2 large oranges

1/4 cup olive oil

1/4 cup lemon juice

1/2 cup chopped parsley

2 green onions or scallions, finely sliced

3 tablespoons chopped fresh mint leaves

2 tablespoons capers, rinsed, drained, and coarsely chopped

2 tablespoons orange zest

1 teaspoon lemon zest

1 teaspoon crushed red pepper flakes

Salt and pepper to taste

DIRECTIONS:

- Peel and trim the ends from each orange.

- Now cut out the orange segments. Using a paring

knife, cut along the membrane on both sides of each segment. Free the segments and add them to a medium sized bowl.

- Add the olive oil, lemon juice, parsley, scallions, mint, capers, orange zest, lemon zest and pepper flakes. Toss lightly and season with salt and pepper.

This is as special occasion recipe since it has quite a few carbs. If you're trying to lose weight, skip this for now.

FOR THE PARMESAN BUTTER SAUCE:

For each serving, melt 2 tablespoons of butter over medium heat in a small saucepan.

Add 2 tablespoons of grated Parmesan and 1/4 cup of heavy cream.

Heat gently until the mixture comes almost to a boil and has started to thicken.

Remove from the heat, season with salt and pepper, and serve over the salmon.

FOR SPICY MAYO:

The idea here is to make a spicy sauce to hide the salmon taste if you don't like it. To do that you need to add something really flavorful. Here are a couple of ideas:

- Mix in some Sriracha Sauce. This is very hot and spicy, so add to taste.

- Mix in some lemon juice and chopped garlic. If you love garlic, this sauce is for you.

- Mix in some seafood sauce. The combination of ketchup and horseradish will add a great flavor to the mayo.

ORANGE CHICKEN

This is a very tasty way to use oranges without overdoing the carbs. Cooking the chicken in the slow cooker infuses all the meat with the orange flavor.

Makes 4 servings

. . .

INGREDIENTS:

1 lb. Chicken tenders or boneless chicken cut up into strips

4 garlic cloves minced (or 1/2 teaspoon garlic powdero

1 teaspoon dried oregano

1 cup orange juice

1 tablespoon grated orange zest

1 tablespoon chopped fresh parsley

Salt and pepper to taste

DIRECTIONS:

- Wash the chicken pieces and dry with a paper towel. Put them into your slow cooker.

- Sprinkle with salt, pepper, garlic and oregano

- Add the orange juice and zest and cover.

- Cook on low for 5 hours until the chicken is very tender.

- Divide into 4 portions, sprinkle with parsley, and freeze.

I USUALLY SPRINKLE some more orange zest over the chicken just before serving to give it even more orange flavor.

SPAGHETTI WITH MEAT SAUCE

Another great dish that just improves with age. With all these servings, this is a great choice for an impromptu casual party, especially in cold winter months. Just add a large green salad and maybe some berries and cream for dessert.

. . .

MAKES 8 servings

INGREDIENTS:
   1 lb. Ground beef
   1 lb. hot Italian sausage (Mild if you don't like your sauce too spicy)
   4 cups sliced mushrooms
   2 cups chopped onion
   2 tablespoons of olive oil
   4 cloves of garlic chopped fine
   2 – 14.5 oz cans of crushed tomatoes
   1/4 cup of tomato paste (approx. a small can)
   2 cups of red wine
   2 tablespoons Italian seasoning
   2 chopped green Jalapeno peppers or 1 teaspoon or more crushed hot peppers (to taste)

DIRECTIONS:
   - Remove the skins from the sausages, then brown the sausage meat in a large skillet. Put into your slow cooker.
   - In the same skillet, brown the ground beef and put into your slow cooker.
   - Add the olive oil, onion, garlic and mushrooms to the skillet and cook a couple of minutes over medium heat until the onions are translucent. Add to the slow cooker.
   - Add the rest of the ingredients to the slow cooker, give it a quick stir, and cook on low for 8 hours or on high for 5 hours.
   - When ready, cool, divide into individual meal portions, and freeze.

·   ·   ·

IF YOU DON'T HAVE a slow cooker, you can make it in a large saucepan on your stove. Follow the directions and cook, covered, on low heat for a couple of hours, checking to make sure it doesn't burn. Add some water if it starts to look very dry.

IF YOU DON'T DRINK the rest of the red wine, you can freeze it for next time. Just pour it into a freezer container, and make sure to allow at least half an inch for expansion when frozen.

THIS SAUCE IS great served over Miracle Noodles or Zucchini Noodles.

TACO BEEF

The key to this recipe is having a good Taco seasoning mix.

You have to be careful when you buy this because some of them are full of sugar and chemicals. Use a reputable spice store. (There are several online)

. . .

INGREDIENTS:

 1 lb. ground beef

 1 cup water

 3 tablespoons taco seasoning

DIRECTIONS:

- Put the ground beef into a large skillet over high heat and brown, mixing occasionally, until all the meat is browned.

- Turn down the heat to low, add the water and seasoning, mix well, then leave the mixture to cook down until all of the water has been absorbed.

- Cool, divide into 4 portions, and freeze.

- To serve, thaw and reheat in a small skillet over medium heat (Or in the microwave.).

- Serve with a side salad with avocado or guacamole and a sprinkling of grated Cheddar.

PULLED PORK & ZUCCHINI NOODLES

You won't believe that a tasty dish like this one can be made so easily.

Makes 8 servings

. . .

INGREDIENTS:

 2 to 3 lb. Pork roast (the fattier the better)
 1 cup of low-carb barb. sauce

DIRECTIONS:

 - Wash and dry your pork roast with paper towels. Place it into you slow cooker, cover it with the barb. sauce, and turn it on low.

 - Cook for 6 hours. When the meat is starting to fall apart, take it out onto a large plate, then pull it apart with a couple of forks. Replace the pulled pork back into the slow cooker and mix it with the juices.

 - Cook for another hour or until all the juices have been reabsorbed back into the meat.

 - Cool, Divide into individual portions, and freeze.

ZUCCHINI NOODLES

THESE ARE a great substitute for regular noodles and a lot lighter tasting. Unfortunately, you can't freeze them, so you'll need to buy a fresh zucchini every time you want to make them, but it's so worth it.

 Makes 1 serving

INGREDIENTS:

 1 large zucchini
 1 tablespoon of butter
 Sea salt and freshly ground pepper

· · ·

DIRECTIONS:

- Using a spiralizer, make the zucchini noodles. You can buy a great spiralizer on Amazon for only $8. Alternatively, you can use a cheese slicer like I do or just a small sharp knife, and just peel off the outside until you hit the seed core.

- Heat a large non-stick pan over medium heat.

- Add the noodles and cook them until just tender. (approx. 1 – 2 minutes) Reduce the heat to low and add the butter. Keep mixing gently until all the noodles are coated. Sprinkle to taste with salt and pepper.

I DON'T WORRY if the butter browns while I'm cooking. It gives it a nice nutty flavor that makes it very tasty.

PEPPERONI & CREAM CHEESE MINI SANDWICHES

These are delicious and really easy to make. Make sure you use a good quality pepperoni and check for added sugar.

INGREDIENTS:

Spicy pepperoni slices

Plain cream cheese

DIRECTIONS:

- Place the pepperoni slices on a piece of doubled paper towel.

- Microwave for 30 seconds.

- Rotate, then microwave another 30 seconds. (The reason you need to rotate is because the slices in the middle won't cook as quickly as the ones by the edge of the microwave turntable.)

When cool, spread with a little cream cheese and top with a second slice of cooked pepperoni.

BERRIES & WHIPPED CREAM

The key here is making a vanilla whipped cream.

- POUR 2 CUPS of heavy or whipping cream into a bowl

with high sides. (This will stop it splashing all over your kitchen.)

- Add a teaspoon of vanilla extract (or 1/4 teaspoon of vanilla powder) 2 tablespoons of sweetener, and a table-spoon of Brain Octane.

- Using an electric egg beater or emersion blender, whip the cream until stiff peaks form.

2 CUPS WILL GIVE you 8 servings - 1/4 cup of whipped cream in each.

LINE A TRAY that will fit into your freezer with non-stick foil or parchment paper. Then divide the cream into 8 little dollops and freeze for half an hour.

Once they are completely frozen you can remove them from the tray, wrap them individually in plastic wrap, then refreeze in a large freezer bag until you need them.

THAW OVERNIGHT in your fridge for use the next day. Serve with 2 tablespoons of berries.

(IF YOU'RE HAVING trouble losing as quickly as you would like, then keep the berry desserts to once or twice a week at most.)

PART FIVE
WHERE TO GET MORE INFORMATION

In this short and sweet guide you have all the information you really need to start the LCHF diet and to be Successful, but I know there are people who would like more information about how LCHF works, what scientific studies have been done, etc.

Also, even though I have been as thorough as possible in my summary of Dr. Eenfeldt's teachings, it is always best if possible to double check with the source.

· · ·

Here is a list of sources that will give you all the extra information you could ever want about Dr. Eenfeldt and about the LCHF diet.

WEBSITE

You can find Dr. Andreas Eenfeldt and all his teachings on LCHF at his website dietdoctor.com

THERE IS a lot of information here for free, but the best information is available to his subscribers.

I cannot recommend enough that you subscribe to this website. For the piddly fee of $9 a month, you get access to a huge amount of information in the form of videos, interviews and courses.

You also have access to several doctors who will answer all your questions on a regular basis.,

THE BEST THING about diet doctor.com is that you know it's completely trustworthy because there are no sponsors and no advertisements.

It's paid for purely by subscriptions, and I think it's very much worth supporting.

VIDEOS

For the best videos, go to diet doctor.com

YOU CAN ALSO SEE lots of videos on Dr Eenfeldt's Youtube channel

BOOKS

Dr. Eenfeld's book is The Low Carb High Fat Food Revolution

WANT MORE BOOKS BY JOANNA ALDERSON?

Check out my website
joannaalderson.com
for Sneak Peeks, recipes and more.

Meanwhile
Turn the page for a full list
and a couple of **FREE** books
to get you started ....

KETO

Keto Series
(8 Books)

BASIC KETO

There are 4 different Keto versions you can choose from:

Simple Keto
Simple Keto after 50
Mediterranean Keto
Keto for Busy People

KETO EXTRAS

And to go with your Basic Diet Plan there are
4 Special Needs books to help you as well.

Keto Miracle Noodles

Keto Egg Fast
Easy Keto Holiday Recipes
Keto Happy Hour Cookbook

Don't want to pay full price for the Extra Books? No problem! Check out this Special Edition .... and SAVE!

FASTING

Keto Fasting Series
(4 Books)

Fasting for Health & Weight Loss
Fasting & The Keto Diet
Keto Fasting A How To Manual

Keto Fasting 3 Books in 1 !

LCHF

LCHF Series
(3 Book)

LCHF A Simple Guide
LCHF Quick & Easy Freezer Plan

LCHF 2 Books in 1 !

DIET & EXERCISE TIPS

Diet & Exercise Tips Series
(2 Books)

How to Lose Weight.... FAST!
How to Lose Belly Fat.... FAST!

Finally I have 6 Special Editions for you.
Each Special Edition includes both Diet & Exercise tip
books .... making each book a complete program!

DIET JOURNALS & PLANNERS

If you've ever had trouble keeping track of your shapeup
progress,
look for my Diet Journals that I created
to go specifically with my books.

They are specially tailored
to your particular diet,
and include all the basics from the book
so you can easily check them.

For your convenience
they come in 2 sizes:
7" x 10"
(almost letter size for your briefcase)
and 5 " x 8 "
(the perfect half-page size for your purse or bag)

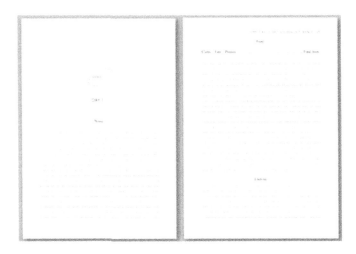

There's lots of room for listing what you eat, for adding
notes, a special section where you can keep track of your
exercise ....

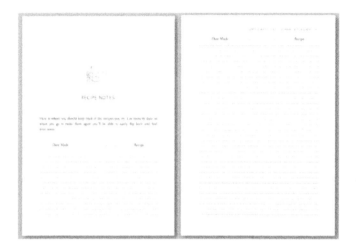

.... and there are even special pages
for notes on the recipes you've tried,
so you can easily reference these again.

At the end of each month you can summarize how you did
that month,
set goals for the next month,
and even put in some photos if you wish.

Each Journal gives you space
for 3 months of records
.... more than enough time
to create a healthy new eating habit!

You don't have to use a Journal to be successful,
but the Experts all agree that doing so
greatly improves
your chances for Success!

Like a couple of **FREE** bookc?

If you're just starting Keto, or
considering starting
but have no idea how,
SIMPLE KETO FOR BEGINNERS
has all the info. you'll need to get going.

And if you're looking to make some changes in your life
and need some inspiration,
or if you're going through some bad times
and need something to cheer you up,
SIMPLE PLEASURES is for you.
It's full of great tips and tricks
that you can easily incorporate into your life,
and it's a quick read.
Get it here.

(If you're reading a print version of this book just go to
www.joannaalderson.com to get the links)

Sign up for my mailing list and
I'll send you these books absolutely **FREE**!

And don't worry.
I'll only email you when I have something good to offer you
like a new book, a **FREE** extra, or a **FREE** promotion,
and of course you can unsubscribe at any time.

ROMANCE ANYONE?

Harriet Pope
Romance Writer

Do you enjoy Romance books?
Are you sick of all the sugary foods & snacks they
encourage?

Try some of my KETO Romance Novels
and meet a couple of tall, dark, handsome,
.... and incredibly sexy Keto doctors!

Sexy and *Healthy* Romance Heros
.... what a concept!

I write Romance novels
under my pen name Harriet Pope at
www.harrietpope.com

If you go to my website you'll find a full list of all my books
plus Sneak Peeks for all of them.

Meanwhile, here's a quick introduction
and a few **FREE** novels for you to try .....

EVERGREEN COVE SERIES

If you like Small Town Romance
with hot sexy heroes
you'll love the Evergreen Cove Series!

Small Town Artist - the first book introduces the Series
& explains why Jessy started to do her house drawings.

Even though there is an order to this Series, all the books can be read as standalone.

Book 1 - Small Town Artist
Jessy & Kevin's story
(A Friends to Lovers Next Door Neighbor Romance).

Book 2 - Small Town Author
Janet & Allan's story
(A Second Chance Later in Life Silver Fox Romance)

Book 3 - Small Town Passions
Mac & Ellen's story
(A Second Chance Later in Life Silver Fox Romance)

Book 4 - Small Town Daddy
Brad & Melanie's story
(An Enemies to Lovers Second Chance Romance)

Book 5 - Small Town Lovers
Alexia & David's story
(A Second Chance Later in Life Silver Fox Romance)

Book 6 - Small Town Inspiration
Steve & Barb's story
(A Friends to Lovers Inspirational Keto Romance)

Book 7 - Small Town Forever Love
Susan & Bob's story
(A Second Chance Later in Life Silver Fox Romance)

Book 8 - Small Town Doctor
Amanda & Seth's story
(An Enemies to Lovers Keto Doctor Boss Romance)

All books are available in ebook and print.

THE FATED SHEIKS TRILOGY

Love to read about
Hot Desert Sands and even hotter
Sexy Desert Sheiks?

try my
Fated Sheiks Trilogy

 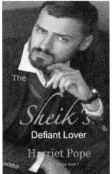 

Book 1 - The Sheik's Reluctant Guest
Sally & Hassim's story
(A Sheik Baby Romance)

Book 2 - The Sheik's Defiant Lover
Belinda & Na'il's story
(A Sheik Enemies to Lovers Romance)

Book 3 - Claimed by the Sheik
Sabrina & Alim's story
(A Sheik Second Chance Later in Life Silver Fox Romance)

To get the full story these books should be read in order

BILLIONAIRE ADVENTURERS

If you enjoy reading about Hot Sexy Powerful Billionaires
who live, love, and travel all over the world,
you'll love the Billionaire Adventurers Series.

These are all stand alone novels
and can be read in any order.

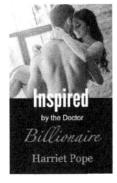 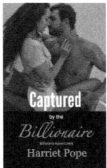 

Inspired by the Doctor Billionaire
Alex & Olivia's story
(A Second Chance Later in Life Keto Doctor Silver Fox
Romance)

Captured by the Billionaire
Carlos & Olivia's story
(An Enemies to Lovers Bandit Romance)

Played by the Billionaire
Elina & Bernard's story
(An Enemies to Lovers Island Romance)

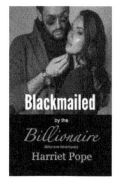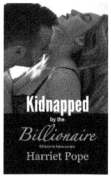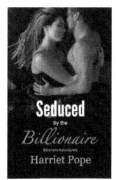

Blackmailed by the Billionaire
Jana & Phill's story
(A Second Chance Enemies to Lovers Later in life Silver
Fox Romance)

Kidnapped by the Billionaire
Reb & Jake's story
(An Enemies to Lovers Biker Romance)

Seduced by the Billionaire
Francois & Ellen's story
(A Second Chance Later in Life Silver Fox Romance)

Like a couple of **FREE** Romance Books?

Small Town Artist is Jessy & Kevin's story
and the introduction to the Evergreen Cove series.
Here is the link.

Inspired by the Doctor Billionaire is the story of
Alex and Olivia and how they ended up in Mexico.
This is the first book in the Billionaire Adventurers series.
Here is the link

(If you are reading a print version of my book, just go to my
website www.harrietpope.com to get the links.)

Sign up for my mailing list
and I'll send you these books absolutely **FREE**!

Don't worry.
I'll only email you when I have something good to offer you
like a new book, a **FREE** extra, or a **FREE** promotion,
and of course you can unsubscribe at any time.

find me at :
www.HarrietPope.com
harrietpope@outlook.com

Printed in Great Britain
by Amazon

37473771R00071